NOVA SCOTIA
PATCHWORK PATTERNS

Instructions and Full-Size Templates for 12 Quilts

Carter Houck

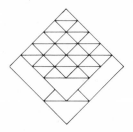

Dover Publications, Inc., New York

Many thanks to the Nova Scotia Museum in Halifax, and to many of its branches; and especially to Scott Robson, Curator and lover of quilts. Thanks also to Donna Garsky and Marleane Rhodenizer for help in finding privately owned quilts and patterns.

Published in Canada by General Publishing Company, Ltd., 30 Lesmill Road, Don Mills, Toronto, Ontario.
Published in the United Kingdom by Constable and Company, Ltd., 10 Orange Street, London WC2H 7EG.

Nova Scotia Patchwork Patterns is a new work, first published by Dover Publications, Inc., in 1981.

International Standard Book Number: 0-486-24145-9
Library of Congress Catalog Card Number: 81-68760

Manufactured in the United States of America
Dover Publications, Inc.
180 Varick Street
New York, N.Y. 10014

INTRODUCTION

The beauty that attracted early settlers to Nova Scotia is still apparent to the visitor who drives through or flies over the country today. Though it has been a settled land since before the *Mayflower* came to Plymouth, it remains a place of small cities and towns, farms, lakes, and woodland.

The French arrived in 1605 and established the first permanent settlement at Annapolis Royal, the second oldest city on the North American continent. Two decades later King James I of England took over the area, granting it a royal coat-of-arms, but the French continued to come to the beautiful farmland they called Acadie, later Acadia. As all readers of *Evangeline* know, most of the Acadians were taken out of Nova Scotia to places from Massachusetts to Georgia, some as far as Louisiana, in the eighteenth century. Only a few years later, during the American Revolution, loyalists fleeing the more southern English colonies (now the United States) came north and settled in Nova Scotia, as did several thousand Blacks prior to the Civil War.

Scotch, Irish, Germans, and English all arrived in the early years of Nova Scotian colonization, each leaving their mark and their names on various parts of the peninsula. The Micmac Indians survived the many European invasions, and their crafts can be seen among the ones brought by the settlers from Europe, and those which originated in this new land. The Nova Scotia Museum celebrates all of the cultural influences in its various locations, stretching from Yarmouth to Cape Breton.

The main branch of the Museum in Halifax is a fine building with both temporary and permanent exhibitions. Quilts and other textiles from their collections are often on temporary display. At other locations throughout Nova Scotia there are farms, homes, and industries preserved as museums. Their invitation is, "Travel through time with the Nova Scotia Museum." For lovers of quilts and other crafts, the spirit of an earlier Nova Scotia is truly brought to life.

The early quilts of Nova Scotia do not reflect the elaborate taste of sections of the eastern United States—they are more like what the people in Maine call "common quilts," practical, economical, and warm. Most were used up or worn out, so that nothing remains from before 1810. The nineteenth-century ones that do remain are simple in design, often *Four-Patch* and *Nine-Patch*. The fabrics are sometimes wools and heavy cottons, obviously left over from family clothing. In the Wile Carding Mill Museum at Bridgewater there is a large fluffy wool quilt batt, just what must have been used in many of those early warm bed covers.

Even though the quilts were utilitarian, they were planned with a good eye for color and arrangement. The simplest squares or square-and-triangle patterns were worked in so many alternative ways that it is often hard to realize that two quite different designs are made from the same pieces. Obviously a pattern would appear in a community, be passed on to a neighbor who would change it and pass it to another neighbor who would change it again. One way in which the designs were varied was in the setting together of the blocks. A favorite way in Nova Scotia is to "hang" the blocks on the diagonal; another is to use a herringbone set, which keeps a geometric design from becoming static; see p. 6.

Eventually more decorative quilts were made in leisure time—what one Nova Scotian referred to as "Sunday quilts." She said her mother made quilts to keep the family warm, but that she had favorites, especially the *Basket* on p. 14, which she made for the spare room or as a gift.

Appliqué appears in some later quilts, a sure sign of prosperous and relaxed times. Flowers, leaves, wreaths, all the components of the delicate and decorative quilts of Baltimore, Philadelphia, and the southern states, were popular in Nova Scotia in the late nineteenth century.

An excellent group of quilts has been brought together in the Nova Scotia Museum in Halifax, through the efforts of the history section and the generosity of interested citizens. Many others, not in the museum, have also been recorded on slides by Scott Robson for use in illustrated lectures. This book does not contain exact copies of any of these Nova Scotia quilts, but does feature block patterns and settings seen throughout the museums and among some quilts and patterns still in private hands.

The simplest of the designs are highly suitable for woolens and other heavy fabrics. Soft-hued cotton prints are in keeping with the intricate pieced geometric designs. Bright colors, largely solid red and green on white, are true to the original appliqués.

Very few of the Nova Scotia quilts have borders. Alternating plain blocks, herringbone sets, and edge-to-edge arrangements simplify the job of computing the size of the quilt. Sashes and sometimes borders appeared more often in later quilts. Edges can be bound, as was usually done in the original early quilts, or borders may be added to change size or modernize the appearance.

Planning for Size and Fabric. Any block design can be used to create a quilt of almost any size—to within a few inches. Some, like the pieced *Giant*

Tulip on p. 26, must conform to a certain number of repeats of the pattern. A border could be used to increase the size a little bit, but not as much as by another complete repeat.

Designs like the *T-Square* on p. 16 are always set with the blocks edge-to-edge and square to the bed, so figuring the number of blocks is a simple matter of dividing the finished block dimensions into the desired finished quilt size. Blocks "hung" diagonally must be measured across from corner to corner for an estimate of length and width requirements; alternating solid color blocks of the same size are often used with these *(Figure 1)*. The same measuring system applies to diagonal or "hung" blocks with a herringbone set, but a slight adjustment must be made at the ends of the strips.

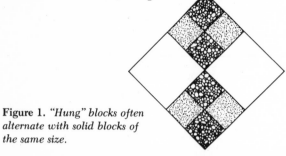

Figure 1. *"Hung" blocks often alternate with solid blocks of the same size.*

Either square or diagonal blocks can be set together with sashes (fabric "frames" surrounding each block) or sashes combined with corner blocks, reducing the number of blocks needed for the total size. Most sashes are 2″ to 3″ wide. Borders can also be used to add width and length.

There are certain basic measurements that will help in planning a quilt.

Mattress sizes are as follows:

Crib	27″ x 52″
Youth	33″ x 66″
Single	30″ x 75″
	33″ x 75″
Twin	39″ x 75″
Long twin	39″ x 80″
Three-quarter	48″ x 75″
Full or double	54″ x 80″
Queen	60″ x 80″
King	76″ x 80″

Fabrics come in fairly standard widths, though there are variations. The following are the most usual:

Cottons and blends	45″
English cottons	36″
European cottons	39″
Decorator fabrics	45″ or 54″
Woolens	54″ or 60″
Hand-loomed woolens	28″

Unbleached muslin comes in many widths, from 39″ to about 80″, usually called sheeting.

Every quilter has her own favorite way of determining the width and length of a quilt for a specific bed, and of estimating fabric amount. To plan the size, the following must be taken into consideration:

- Mattress dimensions.
- Height of bed from floor.
- Whether the quilt is to fall almost to the floor.
- Whether the quilt is to be used as a coverlet with a dust ruffle or spread.
- Whether the quilt is to cover the pillows, or shams are to be used.

All of these specifications must be taken into account for a custom-fitted quilt. If a quilt is being made for sale or some vague future use, the best all-around dimensions are 100″+ long by 80″ to 90″+ wide. These measurements will work as full covers on the narrower beds or as coverlets on the wider ones. If there is no up, down, or sideways in the design, it may also be used the long way across on a king-size bed, with the addition of pillow shams.

There are two approaches to estimating the amount of fabric needed for a quilt. Since Nova Scotia quilts rarely have sashes and borders, estimates here are for the blocks only. No matter which system you use, always add a little extra fabric for safety.

The first system may be used for pieced designs and is the only safe way for appliqué. Decide how many pieces are needed in each color for each block; cut paper pieces to represent these. Lay out all of the pieces for one color in one block as economically as possible without crowding *(Figure 2)*. Measure the area covered and multiply by the number of blocks in the quilt. Example: if all the pieces of one color for one block will fit in a 12″ x 15″ area, then nine blocks will require 1 yard of 45″-wide fabric. Repeat with each color.

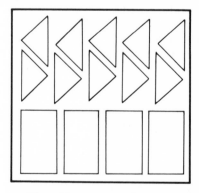

Figure 2. *To measure yardage, lay out all of the pieces for one color in one block as economically as possible without crowding.*

The other system is to start with the finished size of the quilt, then estimate what proportion is to be in each color. The process is at its simplest with a two-color quilt like *T-Square*, p. 16, but can be used with other geometric designs. Start with the fact that 6 yards of 45″ fabric, cut in two and seamed, makes a piece slightly under 90″ wide, and over 100″ long, or the size of most quilts. Piecing means that you will need extra fabric for seams and there will be some waste, so 8 yards would be a safe estimate. For *T-Square*, for instance, that means 4 yards of each color.

Estimating yardage for a scrap-bag quilt requires the ability to be flexible in your thinking. You can always buy extra small pieces that blend. It usually works out like the bread and jam, so that after you finish one quilt, you have to start yet another.

If you plan to use borders, be sure to buy enough length, usually 3 yards, to cut the long side border in one piece. Complete end and side borders up to 10" wide will come out of that length of 45" fabric.

Many people find all of this easier if they use graph paper or big sheets of brown paper and draw the entire quilt to scale. 1" to 1' is a practical proportion. If sashes and borders are to be used, you will also be able to see whether your planning looks as well in actuality as it did in your head. Always remember to add in extra fabric for seams and safety.

Patterns and Cutting. Absolute rules are about as useless in making quilts as they are in raising children. Each person works differently and there are many variables that have to be taken into account. For instance:

• Woolens and other loosely woven fabrics may require slightly wider seams than lightweight cotton and blends.

• Though the longest edge of the pattern piece is usually laid on the straight grain of the fabric, there are times when it is better to have a bias line meet a straight one for stability—experiment and find out ahead of time.

• In using stripes and plaids, grainline is as important to the final design as to the stability of the piecing.

• Though seams are usually pressed all one way in pieced quilts, there may be times and places for pressing seams open to avoid bulk, especially when using heavy fabric.

• Machine piecing can save time if the pieces are large enough and the maker skilled in handling a machine. Sometimes hand piecing saves both time and frustration.

With all of these possibilities in mind, start with the simplest type of design and make it as easy to handle as possible in every way. The fewer the pieces and the less involved the setting, the better.

Choose the easiest fabric to handle—100% cotton in a calico or percale weight is ideal. Preshrink the fabric by dipping it in warm water and letting it drip dry over the shower bar or some other perfectly stable surface. Press it, being sure to pull it if necessary to straighten the grain. (See any good sewing book for a full description of grainline, how to recognize and how to straighten.)

Cut the pattern templates on the broken lines. Position them on the wrong side of the fabric, holding each piece down firmly and drawing around the edge with a medium dark pencil. If you are a real beginner, make another set of templates in the same weight of paper, but without seam

allowances. Center these on each piece and mark again. You now have a penciled seamline on which to stitch. To keep boredom from getting the best of you, mark a number of pieces, say twenty, cut them, then mark some more.

Plastic kitchen bags make marvelous containers for the cut pieces. Sort by color, shape, etc., for easy identification.

Assembling and Stitching. Piecing is usually done a block at a time, though some few patterns are continuous. We are only dealing with blocks in this book. In each pattern description you will find suggestions for the order in which the pieces are to be joined together to make a single block. Pin the pieces right sides together, carefully matching seamlines from corner to corner (*Figure 3*). Stitch by machine (about ten stitches to the inch) or with a running stitch by hand (*Figure 4*); the smaller the running stitches, the better they will hold. As patched pieces are joined together, it is wise to take a small backstitch at the corner intersections (*Figure 5*). Seams should be pressed to one side and toward the darker fabric, before second seams are sewn across them (*Figure 6*).

Figure 3. *Pin the patchwork pieces right sides together, carefully matching seamlines from corner to corner.*

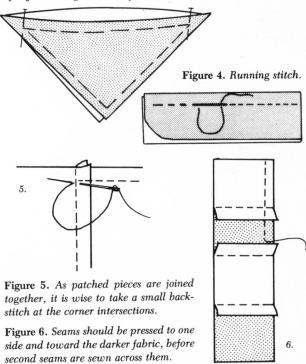

Figure 4. *Running stitch.*

Figure 5. *As patched pieces are joined together, it is wise to take a small backstitch at the corner intersections.*

Figure 6. *Seams should be pressed to one side and toward the darker fabric, before second seams are sewn across them.*

For appliqué cut the background blocks to the finished dimensions plus seam allowances. If you wish, trace the arrangement lightly on the block using dressmaker's carbon and a knitting needle or tracing wheel. Lay all the appliqué pieces in place on the background and pin. Baste them down about ½" away from the raw edges (*Figure 7*). Turn the raw edges ¼" under and using matching thread, sew to the background with a small blind stitch (*Figure 8*); use your fingers and the point of the needle to turn the edges as you go. Clip the sharp corners and take two extra stitches there to prevent raveling (*Figure 9*). It is sometimes necessary to clip the convex curves slightly, especially when using heavy fabric (*Figure 10*). Be sure to remove the basting when you are done.

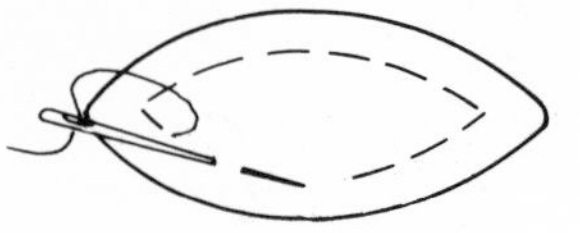

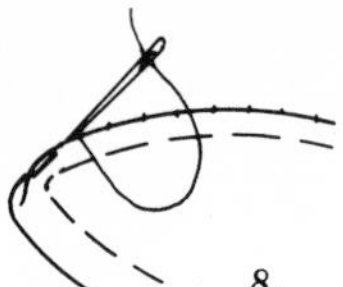

Figure 7. Baste appliqué to the background ½" away from the raw edges.

Figure 8. Turn the raw edges ¼" under and using matching thread, sew to the background fabric using a small blind stitch.

Figure 9. Clip the sharp inward corners and take two extra stitches there to prevent raveling.

Figure 10. Clip the convex curves slightly, especially when using heavy fabric.

Once all the blocks are made and pressed, assemble them in the way you have chosen. Edge-to-edge settings, square to the bed, require nothing more than being matched neatly in long strips. With right sides facing, pin the strips together so that the cross seams match neatly (*Figure 11*), then sew each strip in turn until the entire top is completed.

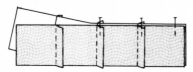

Figure 11. With right sides facing, pin the strips together so that the cross seams match neatly.

"Hung" blocks are set together in much the same way, except that the rows must be planned diagonally and in increasing and decreasing lengths, with half blocks at the ends and on the sides. The last piecing at each of the four corners of the quilt will have a quarter block. The arrangement should be made so that only the solid-color blocks are halved or quartered (*Figure 12*).

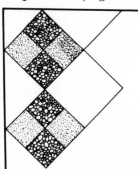

Figure 12. "Hung" blocks are set together with half blocks at the ends and on the sides, and quarter blocks at the corners; only solid color blocks should be halved or quartered.

When blocks are "hung" with herringbone, the long strips are made by sewing one triangle to the upper right and lower left of each block, then sewing this piece to one like it until the desired quilt length is achieved (*Figure 13*). At the top and bottom of the quilt, the blocks in one row and the triangles in the next row must be halved to straighten the edge. In joining the strips, be sure that the point of each block touches the intersection of the triangles (*Figure 14*).

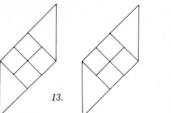
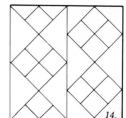

Figure 13. When blocks are "hung" with herringbone, one triangle is sewn to the upper right and lower left of each pieced block, then this piece is sewn to one like it until the desired length is achieved.

Figure 14. In joining "hung" strips, be sure that the upper and lower points of each block touch the intersection of the triangles.

If sashes and corner blocks are used, the pieced or solid-color blocks will be set together with a matching length of sash between each to form rows. These rows are joined with strips made up of alternating sash and corner block pieces. The wide rows of blocks and sashes are joined alternately to the narrow strips of sashes and corner blocks to make the quilt top (*Figure 15*).

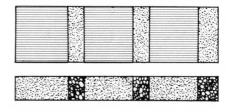

Figure 15. The wide rows of blocks and sashes are joined alternately to the narrow strips of sashes and corner blocks to make the quilt top.

Borders can be added first at the ends, then along the sides (*Figure 16*). For a professional looking border, miter the corners (*Figure 17*).

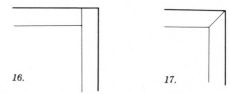

Figure 16. Borders can be added first at the ends, then along the sides.

Figure 17. For a professional looking border, miter the corners.

Final Steps. The last steps in making a quilt are: layer it with batting and backing, quilt it with small stitches, and finish the edges. Batting can be cotton, synthetic, or wool. It comes in large rolls, from crib size to king size and now in an extra-thick type. Backing can be made of two pieces of fabric seamed together or of a bed sheet—seamless. All-cotton is easiest to handle, but washing and rinsing with a softener will improve some of the stiffer blends.

The backing and batting should be slightly larger than the top. Lay the backing flat on the floor or a large table. Lay the batting smoothly on it. The top should lie evenly, but not tightly, on the batting. Start at the center and pin through all layers, working outward toward the sides and corners. Be careful not to stretch or rearrange the fabric.

After the layers are pinned together, baste as shown through all three layers until the entire quilt is held firmly together (*Figure 18*). It can then be quilted on a large frame, a smaller standing oval frame, or a lap frame. The actual quilting is done with small straight running stitches. There is much controversy among quilters about the relative merits of working more quickly with a true running stitch or working more precisely, up and down, one stitch at a time. The answer is to try both ways and see which one works best for you. *Figure 19* on page 32 shows several quilting designs.

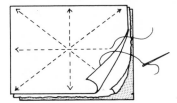

Figure 18. *Baste through all three layers in the direction of the arrows until the entire quilt is held firmly together.*

A quick and simple way to quilt without stitching is the tied or tufted method. Using strong quilting thread or yarn, draw the strand through the backing, batting, and top so both ends are on the quilt top. Then simply tie the ends in a secure overhand knot (*Figure 20*). Tying is usually done at the corners of blocks, and at regular intervals on sashes and borders.

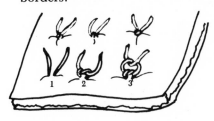

Figure 20. *To tie a quilt, draw the strand up through the backing, batting and top so both ends are on the quilt top (1), then tie the ends in an overhand knot (2, 3).*

The method usually used to finish old quilts was to leave the backing wide enough so that it could be folded over the edge of the batting and the quilt top and finished with a tiny blind stitch on the right side (*Figure 21*). If you want to work in this way you will have to use a backing that makes a pretty edge, and you will need to trim only the batting even with the quilt top.

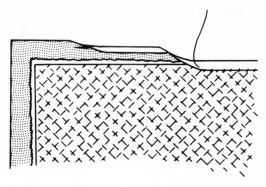

Figure 21. *To finish an edge, leave the backing wide enough to fold over the edge of the batting and top; secure with tiny blind stitches on the right side.*

If a separate binding is used, both the batting and backing must be trimmed. There are two schools of thought on binding—straight grain and bias. Bias is definitely more flexible and in many ways easier to handle. In some prints, stripes, or geometrics, straight grain can be very effective. It will be necessary to piece either type of binding with small seams, always on the straight grain, and pressed open flat.

Because the dimensions of a quilt are slightly smaller after it has been quilted, it should be remeasured to determine the exact length needed. The width of the binding should be four times the planned finished width. Pin the binding carefully, right sides together, along the edges of the quilt, allowing a small pleat at each corner for mitering (*Figure 22*). Stitch a seam by hand or machine, taking up less than one-quarter of the width (*Figure 23*). Turn the binding over the edge, turn the raw edge ¼" under on the wrong side, pin, and blind-stitch in place (*Figure 24*).

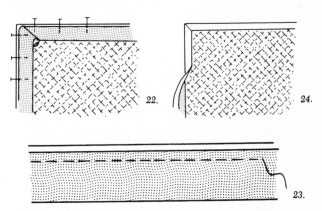

Figure 22. *Pin the binding to the quilt right sides together along the quilt edges, allowing a pleat at each corner for mitering.*

Figure 23. *Stitch a seam by hand or machine, taking up less than one-quarter of the width.*

Figure 24. *Turn the binding over the edge, turn the raw edge ¼" under on the wrong side, pin, then blindstitch in place.*

NINE-PATCH QUILTS

If the blocks are turned on the diagonal, they are said to be "hung." Many early Nova Scotia quilts in very simple designs like *Nine-Patch* and *Four-Patch* were made that way to create a more interesting effect. They were sometimes made in the dark colors of men's work clothes, often wool.

The *Framed Nine-Patch* is a more elaborate and planned version of this old favorite. Maximum effect is created by using a light, medium, and dark fabric throughout so that the medium carries diagonally across the quilt.

TO MAKE "FOUR AND NINE" (HUNG)

Planning. Use scrap-bag pieces, in equal quantities of light and dark or print and solid. Remember that each 6″ block measures 8½″ across from point to point diagonally. A quilt eight blocks across and ten blocks long will measure 68″ x 85″.

Cutting. For each *Nine-Patch* block cut nine squares using Template #1, four in one color value and five in the other. For each *Four-Patch* block cut four squares using Template #2, two in each color value. Cut enough solid triangles using Template #3 to form the border.

Construction. Make up an equal number of each kind of block (it may take a few more of one block than the other, depending on your planning). Lay the blocks out on a large area such as the floor, and keep moving them until you like the color arrangement. Pin and seam them in strips, including the #3 pieces at the ends of each strip—starting with two blocks and two triangles (Row 1), then four blocks and two triangles (Row 2), six blocks and two triangles, etc., to form the diagonal layout. Number the strips and then join them in order, adding two triangles in each corner as shown.

Note. If you use wool fabric and wool or extra-thick batting, you may find it easier to seam the top to the back, leaving the end open like a pillow case to insert the batting. The other choice is to use a lightweight backing such as sateen, bringing it over the edge as a binding ; see p. 7. Tie the quilt just like Grandma did with her heavy wool quilts; (p 7).

TO MAKE "FRAMED NINE-PATCH"

Planning. Each block is 14″ square, with 2″ sashes between, so plan the size accordingly—five blocks across with six sashes measures 82″, six blocks long with seven sashes measures 98″. Approximately one-half of the total fabric will be light, three-fifths dark, and two-fifths medium (p. 4), not including the border, which may be added.

Cutting. For each block:
Template #1	. . .	8 light
Template #1	. . .	9 medium
Template #4	. . .	4 dark
Template #5	. . .	4 light
For sashes:		
Template #6	. . .	light
For corner blocks:		
Template #1	. . .	medium

Construction. Make up the *Nine-Patch* in three strips—join the strips to form the center block, with the medium square in the center and eight light squares around it. Seam a #4 piece to each side. Seam #1 pieces to each end of the other #4 pieces, then seam these strips to the long sides of the first assembly. Continue in the same manner with #5 pieces. When all the blocks are completed, make up sashes with corner blocks. Join as described on p.6. See the inside back cover for a color illustration.

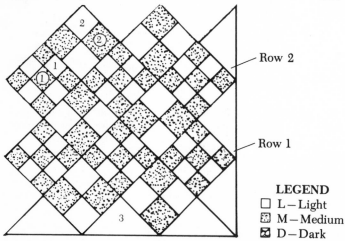

Row 2

Row 1

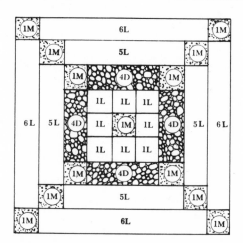

Templates are given on Plates 1 and 2, pp. 33, 36.

SQUARE AND TRIANGLE VARIATIONS

The square and a matching right-angle triangle are the basis of many quilt designs—four-, nine-, or five-patch. The *Rolling Ring* can be seen as a variation of *Shoo Fly* with light sashes and dark corner blocks, or as a continuous edge-to-edge *Robbing Peter to Pay Paul* design.

What we have called *Canada Cross* is a variation of many *Star* or *Cross* designs; it may be set with alternating plain blocks or with sashes. See the inside front cover for a color illustration.

TO MAKE "ROLLING RINGS"

Planning. The templates are given in three sizes, from 1″ to 3″. If you think of the blocks as marked on the diagram, with four squares each way, a complete (sixteen-square) block will measure 4″, 8″, or 12″ square, depending on the templates you choose. Using the 2″ template, nine blocks across will make a 72″ width—add one more row of 2″ for design balance and you will have 74″. Slightly more than one-half of the total yardage will be light, slightly less than half will be dark (p. 4). Add a border if you wish.

Cutting. For each (sixteen-square) block:

Template #1	. . .	7 light
Template #1	. . .	5 dark
Template #2	. . .	4 light
Template #2	. . .	4 dark

Construction. Join the white and dark #2 pieces into squares. Join four squares each into strips to conform to the diagram, then join the four strips into a block. Continue in this way, finally joining all blocks to make the continuous design.

TO MAKE "CANADA CROSS"

Planning. Each block will be 5″, 10″, or 15″ square, depending on what size templates you choose. The 3″ squares, making a 15″ block, can produce a quick-and-easy quilt. You'll need four blocks and five 3″ sashes for width, five blocks and six 3″ sashes for length, for a 75″ x 93″ quilt—borders may be added. Slightly over one-half of the block fabric will be dark, and slightly less than half will be light, excluding sashes and borders.

Cutting. For each block:

Template #1	. . .	5 light
Template #1	. . .	12 dark
Template #2	. . .	8 light
Template #2	. . .	8 dark

Construction. Join the light and dark #2 pieces into squares. Join five squares each into strips to conform to the diagram, then join the five strips into a block. Continue in this way until all blocks are completed. Join the blocks with sashes or alternating solid blocks (p. 6).

LEGEND
☐ L—Light
▨ D—Dark

Templates are given on Plate 3, p. 37.

WINDMILL "HUNG" WITH HERRINGBONE

The perfect beginner's block is a four-patch, cut on the diagonal to form the blades of a windmill. It can be made in two colors, or muslin and scrap-bag pieces in many happy combinations. The addition of the herringbone setting and the "hung" blocks take it out of the realm of the ordinary (p. 6).

Planning. If you use two colors for the block pieces and a third color or muslin for the herringbone pieces, planning should be quite simple. Remember that the 8″ block measures something over 11″ across from point to point diagonally. Eight blocks across by nine blocks long will make a nice 90″ by 100″ (more or less) quilt. The fabric for the herringbone is one-half the total, each of the other two colors are one-fourth (p. 4).

Cutting. For each block:

Template #1	.	.	.	4 light
Template #1	.	.	.	4 dark
Template #2	.	.	.	2 muslin for every pieced block

Construction. Join the light and dark #1 pieces into squares. Join four squares into a block, alternating light and dark, until there are enough blocks for the entire quilt. Make long strips, setting the #2 pieces in as shown in the diagram. Piece the strips together as described on p. 6.

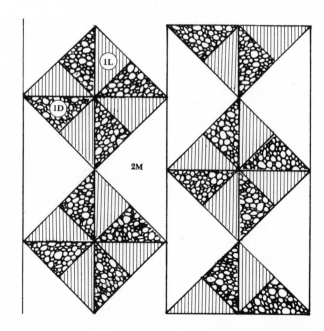

LEGEND
- ▥ L – Light
- ▨ D – Dark
- ☐ M – Muslin

Templates for this quilt are given on Plate 4, p. 40.

BASKET QUILT

Take the basic square and triangle idea a little further—turn the squares into rectangles, and the triangles into larger triangles. The possibilities become limitless. This simplest of all baskets can be seen as piled high with fruit by changing the color values halfway up. The blocks should be "hung" and set with alternating plain blocks, herringbone (p. 6), or sashes.

Planning. Use scrap-bag pieces combined with white, preferably muslin, for the pieced blocks. The sets or sashes should be made in one solid color or small print throughout. In planning for either the alternating blocks or herringbone, remember that the 10″ block measures a bit over 14″ diagonally, from point to point. So, six blocks wide by seven blocks long make a quilt 84″ by 98″ without the border. The alternating blocks or herringbone will make up about one-half the total fabric and the white a little over one-fourth (p. 4).

Cutting. For each block:

Template #1	. . .	1 white
Template #1	. . .	1 dark
Template #2	. . .	2 white
Template #3	. . .	2 dark
Template #3	. . .	15 white
Template #3	. . .	13 medium

Construction. Join all the medium and white #3 pieces into squares and then into strips, following the piecing diagram. Join strips and add the dark #1 piece to form a large square. Join dark #3 pieces to the ends of #2 pieces, seam these strips to the sides of the first square and add the white #1 piece to the corner. Complete the quilt with plain blocks, herringbone sets or sashes (p. 6).

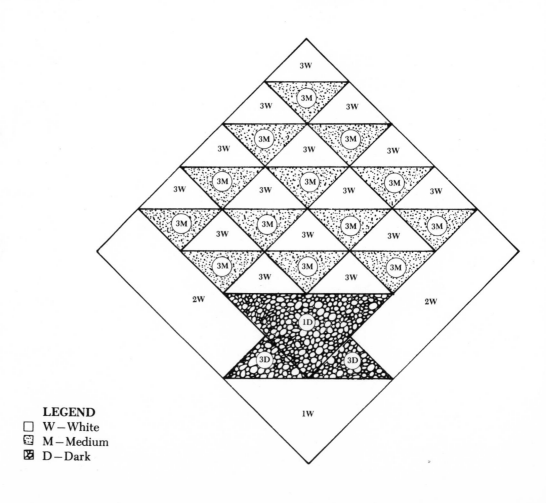

LEGEND
☐ W—White
▨ M—Medium
▨ D—Dark

Templates for this quilt are given on Plate 5, p. 41.

T-SQUARE QUILT

Positive-negative or *Robbing-Peter-to-Pay-Paul* designs are the great optical illusions of quilting. *T-Square* is more complex in its form of trickery than some, but wonderfully simple to make. Shown in this edge-to-edge setting, the formation of the white "T" in the center is obvious.

Planning. Two colors or two values of one color (light and dark) are necessary to make this type of design work. Beyond that, the planning of this quilt is about as easy as planning can get. The blocks are set straight, edge-to-edge, and a border isn't even necessary. The measurements of the finished quilt are multiples of the 9″ blocks. The fabric re-quirements are divided in equal parts of light and dark (p. 4).

Cutting. For each block:

Template #1	.	. .	1 light
Template #1	.	. .	1 dark
Template #2	.	. .	5 light
Template #2	.	. .	5 dark

Construction. Make up five squares of one light and one dark #2 piece each and one large square of one light and one dark #1 piece. Join the squares to make the dark "T," as shown in the diagram. Join the blocks into strips with all "T's" going in the same direction. Join the strips, matching all corners carefully.

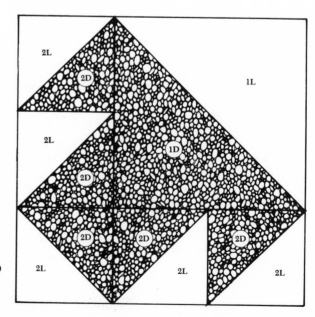

LEGEND
☐ L — Light
▨ D — Dark

16

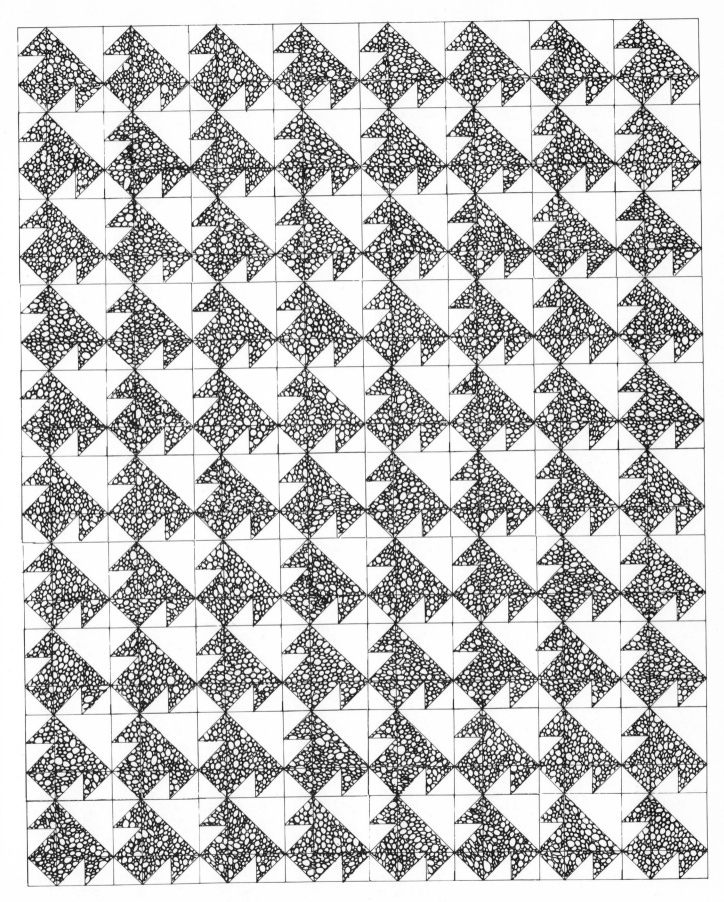

Templates for this quilt are given on Plate 6, p. 44.

JACOB'S LADDER QUILT

A Nova Scotia favorite is this old pattern with its biblical name and intricate arrangement possibilities. A classic joining of the four squares that form the block is shown here, but try turning the squares and changing the color values for other effects.

Planning. Edge-to-edge is the proper way to set the *Jacob's Ladder* blocks so that the design becomes a continuous and winding puzzle. Four 10″ squares make up each block; four blocks by five blocks make a generous size quilt (p. 4). White or muslin makes up one-half the total fabric requirement and the remainder is half-and-half dark and medium. Use two solid colors, two prints, or scrap-bag pieces in two distinct values.

Cutting. For each block:

Template #1	. . .	8 white
Template #1	. . .	4 medium
Template #1	. . .	4 dark
Template #2	. . .	16 white
Template #2	. . .	8 medium
Template #2	. . .	8 dark

Construction. Make up four small squares to form each block, two squares of #1 pieces and two squares of #2 pieces. Join those together in the order shown in the diagram. You can now piece the blocks as illustrated, or try turning them for other effects.

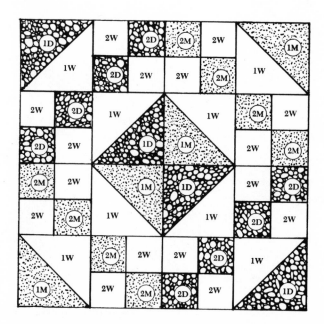

LEGEND
☐ W — White
▨ M — Medium
▨ D — Dark

Templates for this quilt are given on Plate 7, p. 45.

SNOWBALL QUILT

Cut the corners off squares and what do you have—octagons? Yes, but quilters say that you have *Snowballs*. The two variations seen in Nova Scotia were both set alternately with *Nine-Patch* blocks, the total effect varying greatly by a simple reversal of light and dark in that checkerboard block. The *Snowball* block can also be used in a positive-negative or *Robbing-Peter-to-Pay-Paul* arrangement without the *Nine-Patch*.

Planning. The small blocks, 6″ square, are set edge-to-edge, alternating *Snowball* and *Nine-Patch*. Fourteen across and sixteen long will make a full-size quilt, 84″ x 96″. Even though the blocks are small, they are easy to machine-piece for quicker results. Variation A is about one-half light fabric and one-half dark. Variation B is at least three-fifths light and about two-fifths dark. Be sure to allow adequate fabric for the many seams when the blocks are this small.

Cutting. For each *Snowball* block:

Template #1	. . .	1 white
Template #3	. . .	4 dark

For each *Nine-Patch* block, Variation A:

Template #2	. . .	4 white
Template #2	. . .	5 dark

For each *Nine-Patch* block, Variation B:

Template #2	. . .	5 white
Template #2	. . .	4 dark

Construction. Seam the #2 pieces for each block into strips, two in one alternating pattern, one in the opposite. Seam the three strips together to form a checkerboard as shown. Seam the four #3 corners onto the #1 octagon. Make up long strips alternating *Snowballs* and *Nine-Patch*. Plan ahead so that when the strips are joined, the blocks will alternate across the quilt.

LEGEND
☐ W—White
▨ D—Dark

Variation A

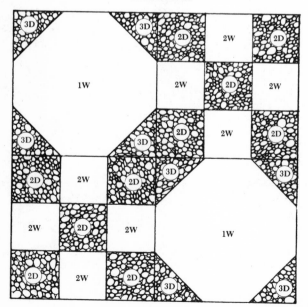

Variation B

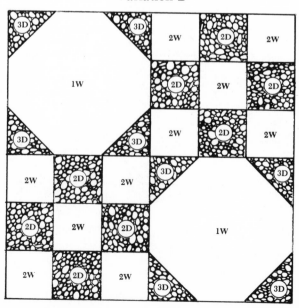

Variation A

Templates for this quilt are given on Plate 8, p. 48.

DUCKS AND DUCKLINGS QUILT

Though four-patch and nine-patch blocks are the most common among the older Nova Scotia quilts, the five-patch followed along for the more adventurous designers in geometric piecing. It is seen here in *Ducks and Ducklings*, a lighter and more playful extension of *Churn Dash*.

Planning. The 10″ block given here can be used with any setting, square to the bed or "hung." It works especially well with the herringbone or with alternating solid color blocks. In either case one-half the fabric of the quilt will be that chosen for the herringbone, and the other half, in two evenly divided colors, will make up the blocks. Remember that the 10″ block measures something over 14″ diagonally across from point to point.

Cutting. For each block:

Template #1	. . .	4 dark
Template #2	. . .	4 light
Template #3	. . .	1 dark
Template #4	. . .	12 light
Template #4	. . .	4 dark

The #5 pieces will be cut for the herringbone sets.

Construction. Joining one dark and one light #4 triangle together first, make up four squares for the corners. Add two light #4 triangles as shown, then add one #1 triangle to each following diagram. Assemble two corner squares and two #2 pieces into two strips; assemble the remaining #2 piece and the #3 piece into a narrow strip. Seam the strips together as shown. For details on setting the blocks with the herringbone, see p. 6.

LEGEND
☐ L — Light
⊠ D — Dark

Templates for this quilt are given on Plates 9 and 10, pp. 49, 52.

WHIRLIGIG QUILT

This marvelous and slightly more involved *Windmill* design actually seems to be in motion when seen in a large quilt. The darks and lights whirl in opposite directions and delight the eye with optical illusion.

Planning. Use three colors or three values of one color, and always use an edge-to-edge setting. It takes four blocks to create the total pattern effect, all made up alike—two in one position and the other two turned so that darks and lights meet. The 8″ blocks make a standard quilt when set ten across and twelve long. One-half the total fabric will be of the medium shade for the #1 square. The other half will be equally divided between light and dark for the triangular #2 pieces.

Cutting. For each block:

Template #1	. . .	1 medium
Template #2	. . .	2 dark
Template #2	. . .	2 light

Construction. Piece the triangles around the square for each block (one-hundred and twenty blocks for the size mentioned above). Seam blocks into strips so that light and dark meet. Seam the strips together so the colors alternate across the quilt as well.

LEGEND
☐ L—Light
▦ M—Medium
▨ D—Dark

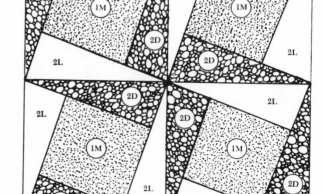

Templates for this quilt are given on Plate 10, p. 52.

GIANT TULIP QUILT

The optical illusions of this gigantic four-square block are delightful. The squares, as shown, join at the base of the stems, with tulips growing out toward each corner, creating secondary designs where they meet with other blocks.

Planning. In the original quilt there are two whole blocks—formed of four squares each—across, and two and one-half blocks in length. The quilt is 82″ by 102½″, without a border. The traditional colors are red and green on white. About three-fifths of the total fabric is white, the other two-fifths evenly divided between green and red.

Cutting. For each 20½″ square (one-quarter of block):

Template #1	.	.	2 green
Template #1	.	.	12 red
Template #2	.	.	5 white
Template #3	.	.	1 white
Template #3	.	.	3 green
Template #4	.	.	5 white

Template #5	.	.	2 white
Template #6	.	.	2 white
Template #7	.	.	1 white

3 yards green bias tape (½″ wide when finished)

Construction. This is a good design for machine piecing, with its large sections and straight lines. Piece the three flowers using red #1 pieces; set them together with the white #2 and #4 pieces, and the #3 green pieces. Assemble the green #1 pieces with the white #2 and #3 pieces in the area on the diagram marked "center of block." Then assemble the entire square using white #5, #6, and #7 pieces. Following the diagram, appliqué the stems in place using green bias tape. Make 20 squares in this manner. To make four blocks, set four sets of squares together so the bases of the stems meet. Then sew the remaining four squares together as one strip. Set four blocks together to form one large square, and then sew the single strip of squares across one edge. Bind the edges of the quilt with white.

LEGEND
- ☐ W—White
- ▦ R—Red
- ▨ G—Green

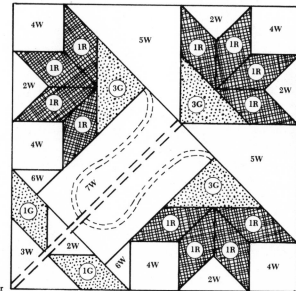

center of block

Templates for this quilt are given on Plates 11–13, pp. 53, 56, 57.

ROSE OF SHARON WREATH

The appearance of this classic floral appliqué is intricate and delicate. The ends of the buds from one block seem to flow into those from the next. In actuality it is a rather simple design, made up from four shapes and a bias circle.

Planning. The original quilt is square, three 18" blocks in each direction, with a wide (about 10") border. The border has a long trailing vine of bias with roses, buds, and leaves along the four sides. The white blocks may be cut larger or one more can be added in each direction. The size of the design can be increased on a larger block by expanding the bias strip circle an inch or so; it is 10" in diameter as shown here. The traditional colors of the quilt are red and green, with a base of white.

Cutting. For each block:
    Template #1 . . . 4 red
    Template #2 . . . 12 green
    Template #3 . . . 12 red
    Template #4 . . . 24 green
    1 white 19" square (includes ½" seam
        allowance)
    24" of green bias tape (½" wide when finished)

Construction. Lay out and pin all pieces in place on the white square, positioning the 10" circle of bias tape first. To make placement easier, use a compass to mark a 10" diameter circle in the center of the block. Baste, turn the edges, and stitch appliqués in place by hand (pp. 5–6). The blocks are seamed together and a border can be added, using the same templates for a trailing vine design. The petals of the roses (indicated by broken lines) are formed by stitching when the quilting is done.

LEGEND
R — Red
G — Green

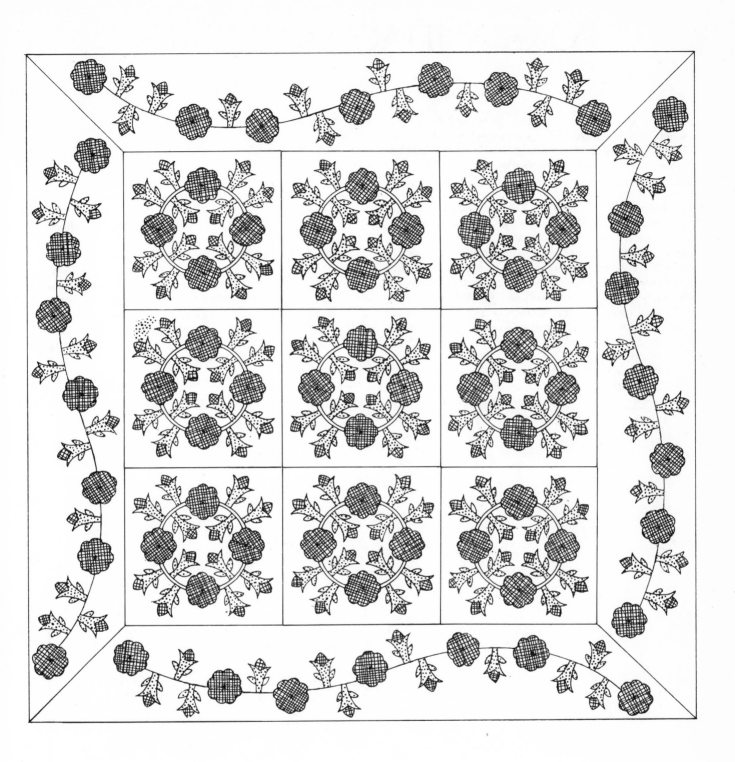

Templates for this quilt are given on Plate 14, p. 60

OAK AND ACORN QUILT

Simpler and bolder than its U.S. cousin, *Oak Leaf Cluster*, this design is an easy project for the novice in appliqué. The pieces are large, the curves not too hazardous, and the effect is eye-catching.

Planning. The pieces, when set on 16″ white squares, will nearly meet at the corners, forming a secondary pattern and a strong diagonal line across the quilt. Five blocks across and six in length make a nice 80″ by 96″ finished piece. The original is bound in narrow green bias. The entire base is white; an almost equal amount of red and green is needed for the appliqué. Lay the pattern pieces on a marked area to figure exact yardage of color for each block —then multiply (p. 4).

Cutting. For each block:

Template #1 . . .	1 red	
Template #2 . . .	4 red	
Template #3 . . .	4 green	

1 white 17″ square (includes ½″ seam allowance)

Construction. Lay out and pin all pieces in place on the white square, positioning piece #1 in exact center first. Baste, turn the edges, and stitch appliqués in place by hand (pp. 5–6). The blocks are seamed together and the edges can be bound with bias tape. Echo quilting (following the shape of the appliqués as in Hawaiian quilts) is suitable, or any plain geometric quilting design (see p. 7) can be used in the white areas.

LEGEND
▦ R — Red
⬚ G — Green

30

Templates for this quilt are given on Plates 15 and 16, pp. 61, 64.

Figure 19
TYPICAL QUILTING DESIGNS

Decorative Designs

Feather Designs

All-over Designs

Narrow Strips and Border Designs

Pattern Pieces For NINE-PATCH QUILTS

PLATE 1

seam allowance

**FRAMED
NINE-PATCH

FOUR-AND-NINE**

Template #1

seam allowance

seam allowance

**FRAMED
NINE-PATCH**

Template #5

place on fold of fabric

**FRAMED
NINE-PATCH**

Template #4

FOUR-AND-NINE

Template #2

seam allowance

seam allowance

33

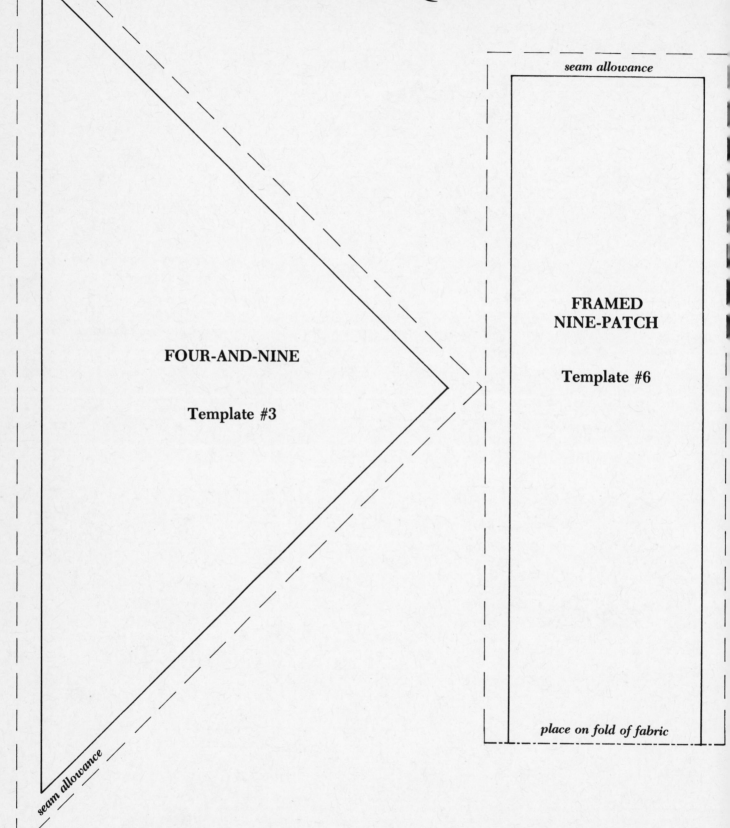

PLATE 2

Pattern Pieces For NINE-PATCH QUILTS

FOUR-AND-NINE

Template #3

seam allowance

FRAMED NINE-PATCH

Template #6

seam allowance

place on fold of fabric

36

Pattern Pieces For
SQUARE AND TRIANGLE VARIATIONS
PLATE 3

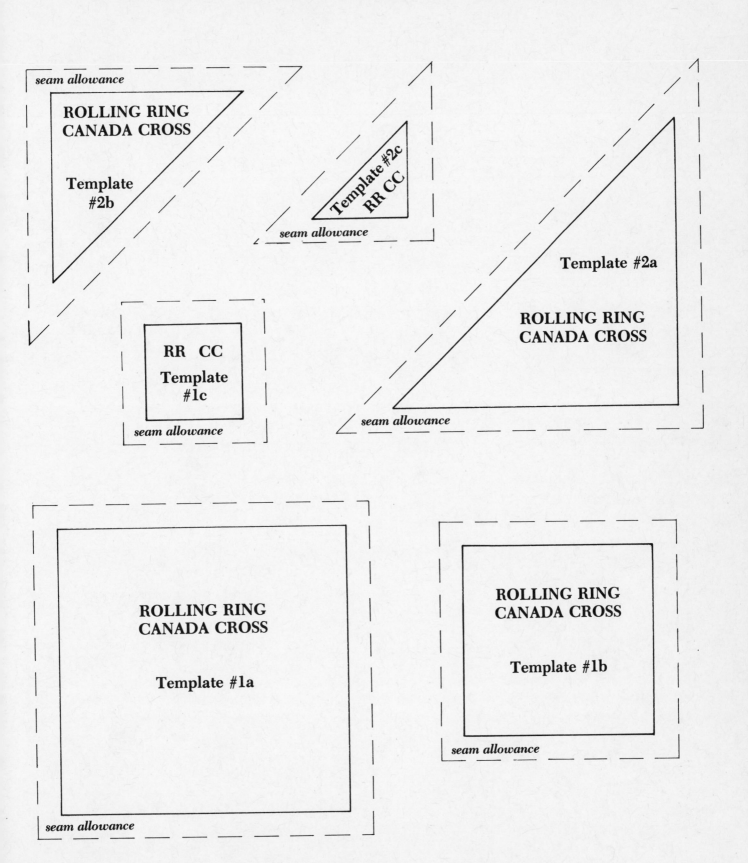

seam allowance

ROLLING RING CANADA CROSS

Template #2b

Template #2c
RR CC

seam allowance

Template #2a

ROLLING RING CANADA CROSS

RR   CC
Template #1c

seam allowance

seam allowance

ROLLING RING CANADA CROSS

Template #1a

seam allowance

ROLLING RING CANADA CROSS

Template #1b

seam allowance

PLATE 4

Pattern Pieces For
WINDMILL "HUNG" WITH HERRINGBONE

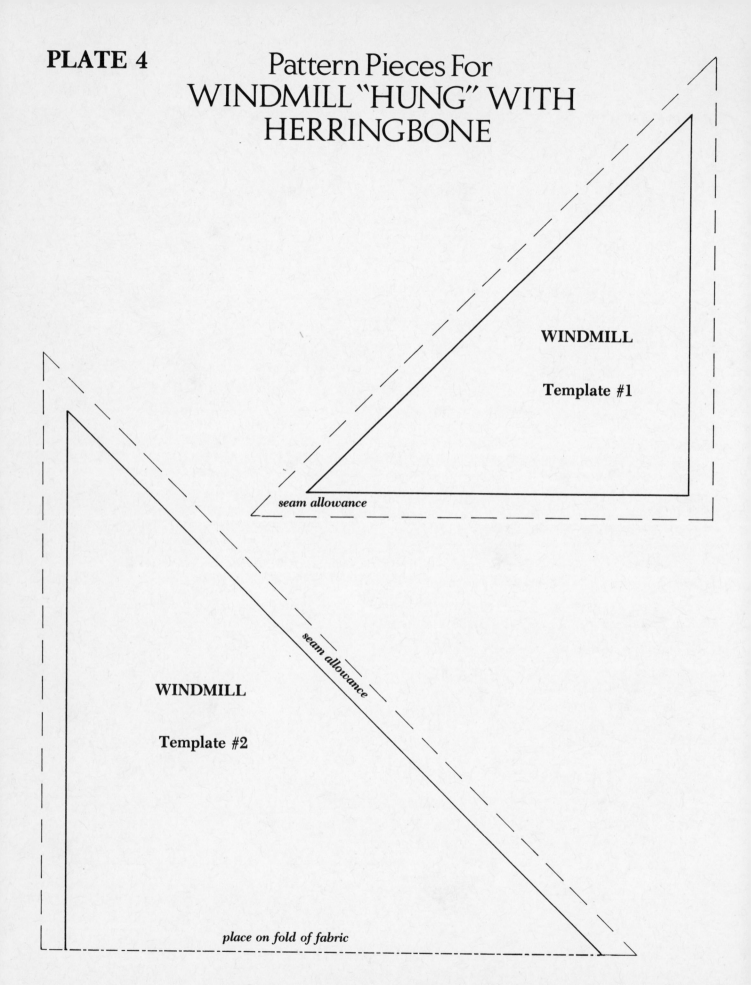

WINDMILL

Template #1

seam allowance

seam allowance

WINDMILL

Template #2

place on fold of fabric

Pattern Pieces For
BASKET QUILT

PLATE 5

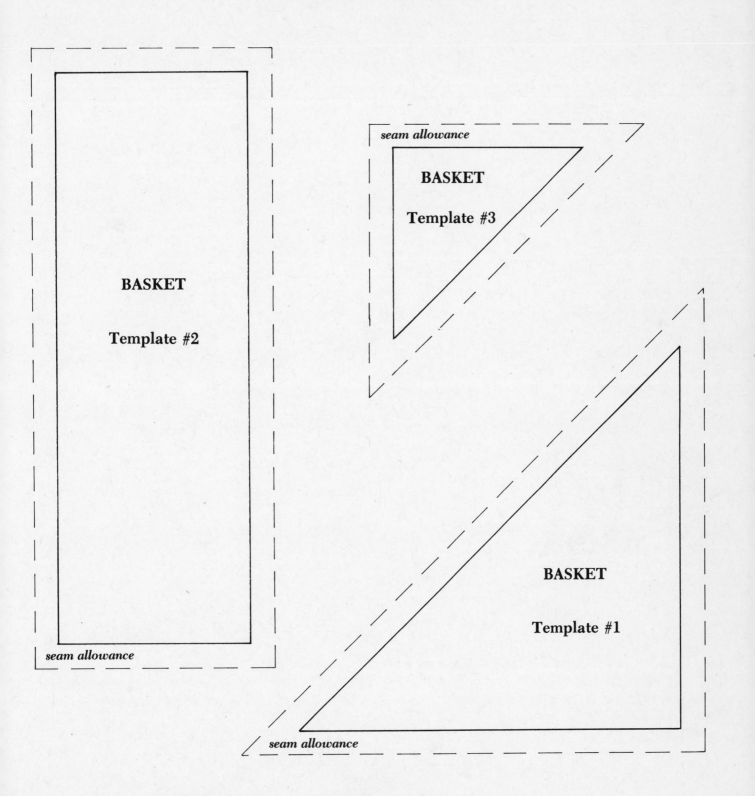

BASKET

Template #2

seam allowance

seam allowance

BASKET

Template #3

BASKET

Template #1

seam allowance

PLATE 6

Pattern Pieces For
T-SQUARE QUILT

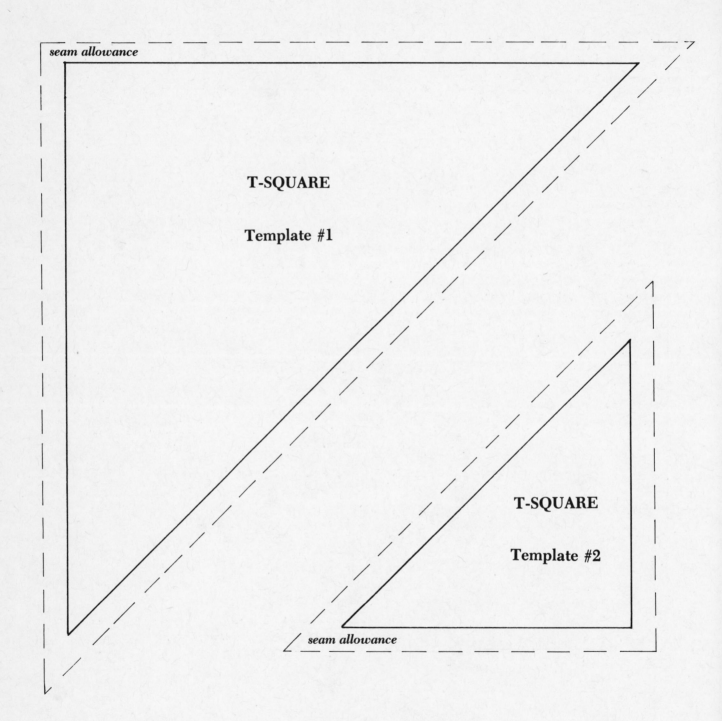

seam allowance

T-SQUARE

Template #1

T-SQUARE

Template #2

seam allowance

Pattern Pieces For
JACOB'S LADDER QUILT

PLATE 7

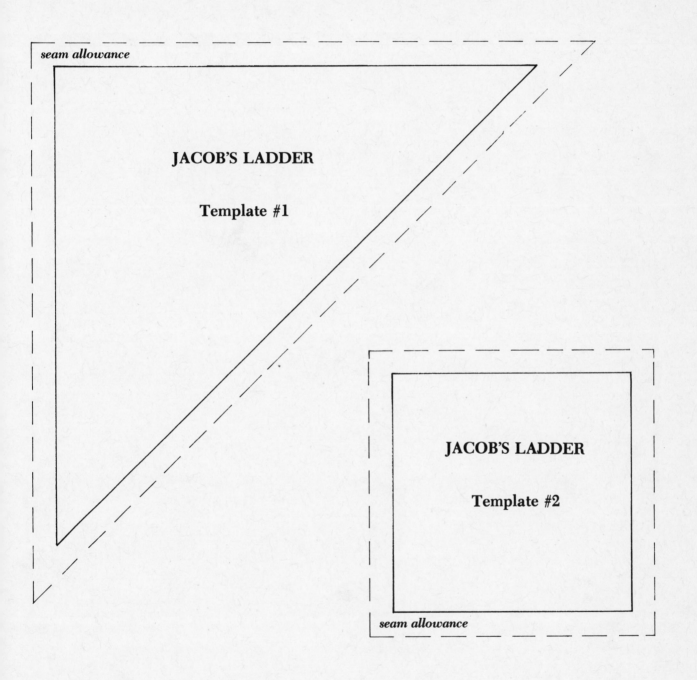

seam allowance

JACOB'S LADDER

Template #1

JACOB'S LADDER

Template #2

seam allowance

PLATE 8

Pattern Pieces For SNOWBALL QUILT

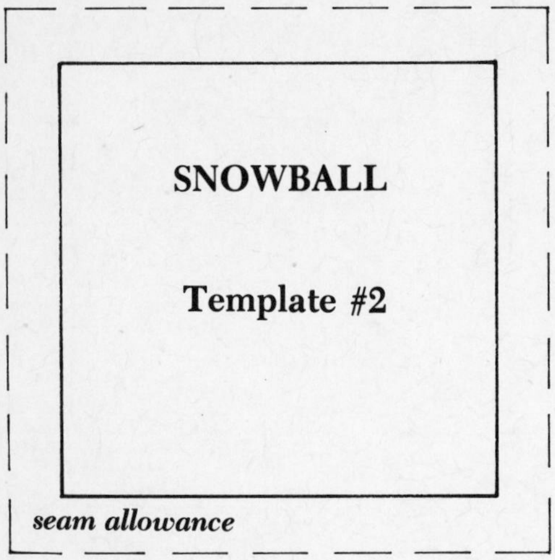
SNOWBALL
Template #2
seam allowance

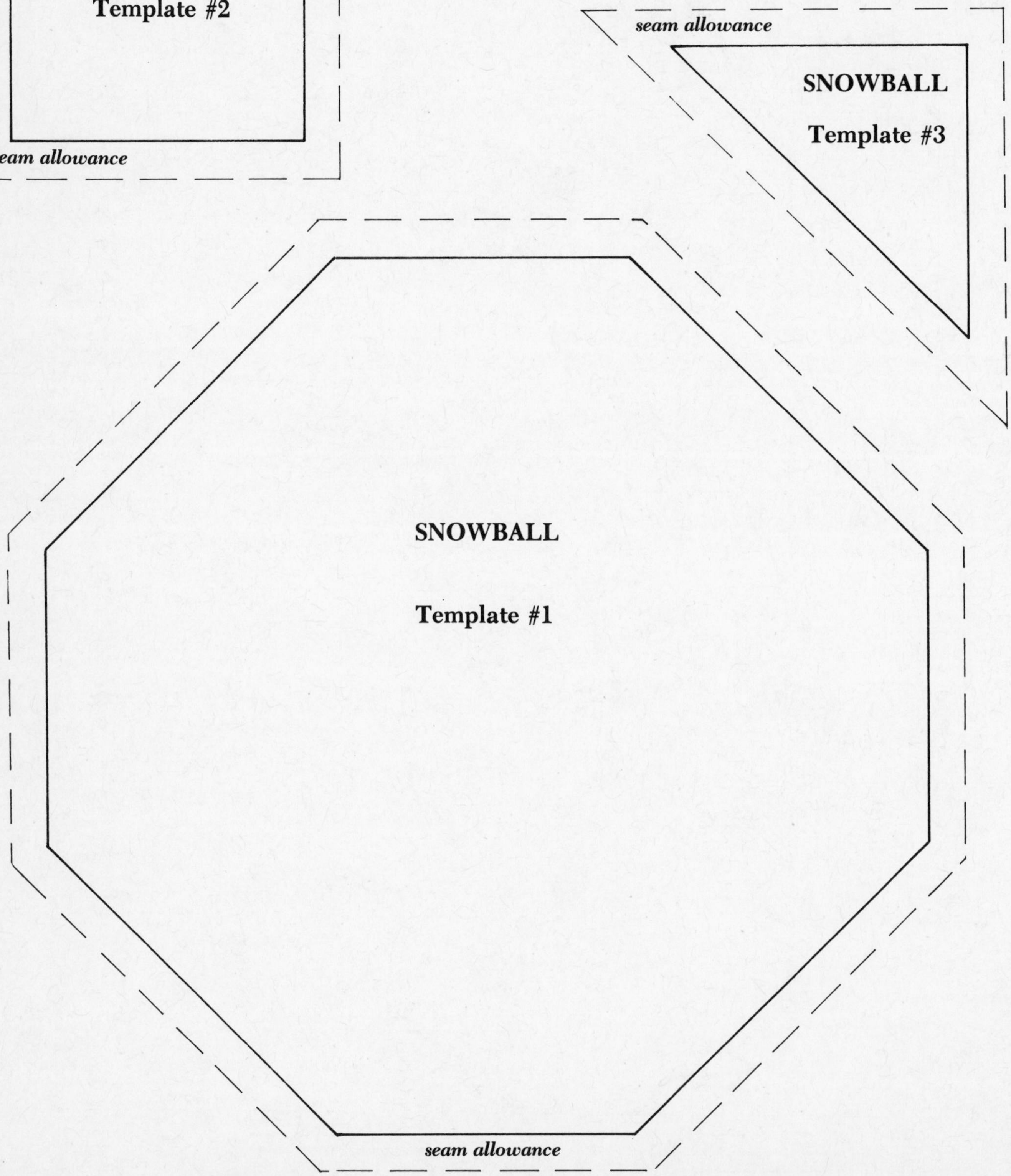
seam allowance
SNOWBALL
Template #3
SNOWBALL
Template #1
seam allowance

Pattern Pieces For DUCKS AND DUCKLINGS QUILT

PLATE 9

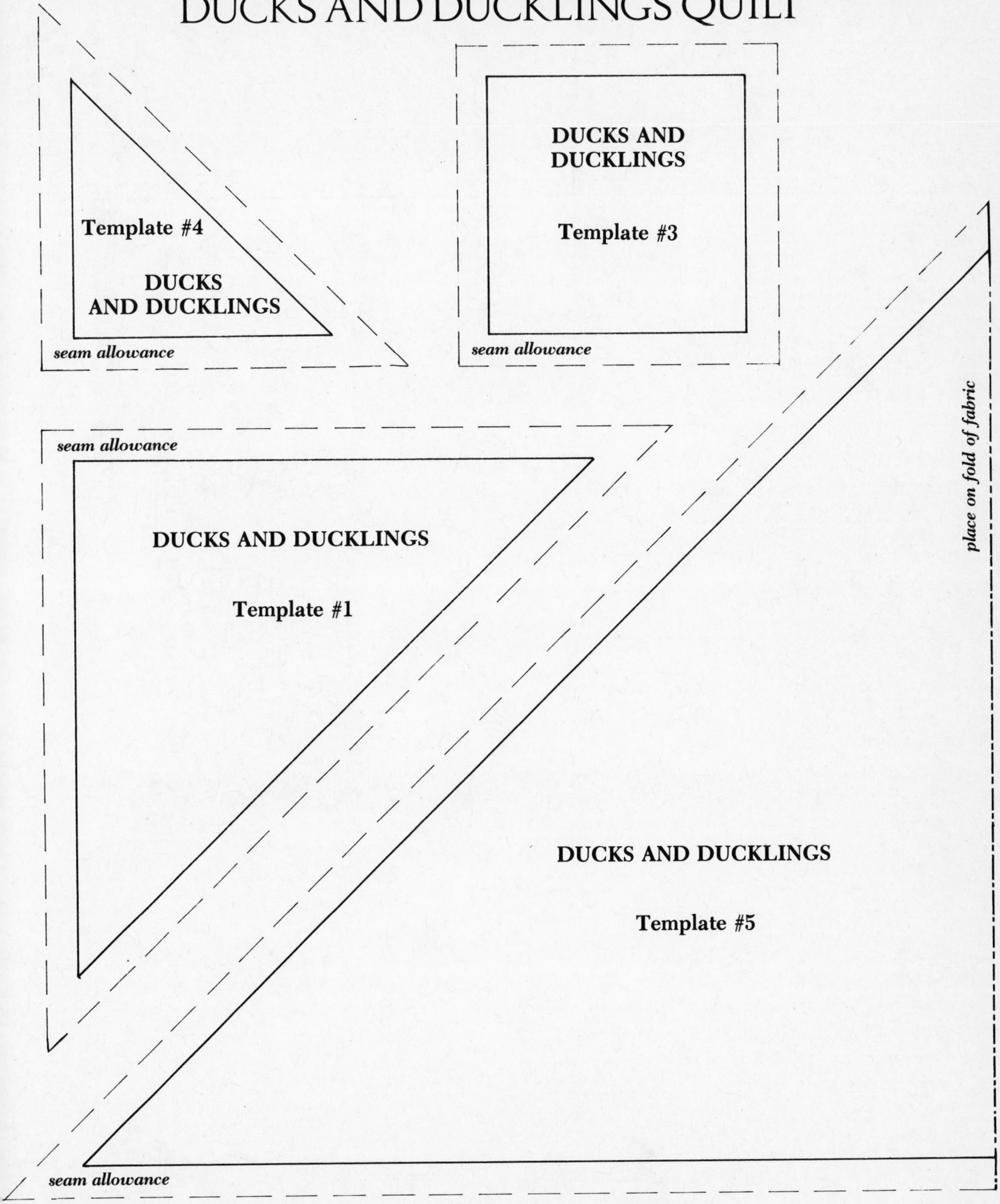
Template #4
DUCKS
AND DUCKLINGS
seam allowance
DUCKS AND
DUCKLINGS
Template #3
seam allowance
seam allowance
DUCKS AND DUCKLINGS
Template #1
place on fold of fabric
DUCKS AND DUCKLINGS
Template #5
seam allowance

Pattern Pieces For
WHIRLIGIG, DUCKS AND
DUCKLINGS QUILT

seam allowance

WHIRLIGIG

Template #2

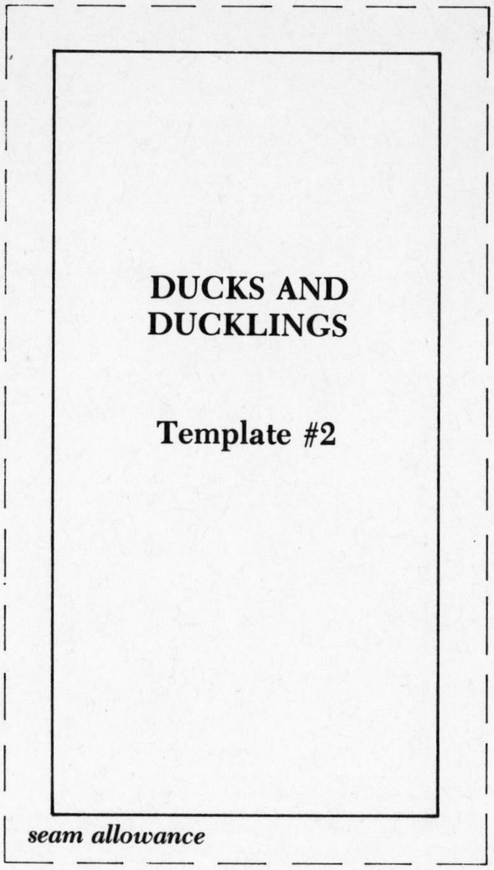

PLATE 10

**DUCKS AND
DUCKLINGS**

Template #2

seam allowance

WHIRLIGIG

Template #1

seam allowance

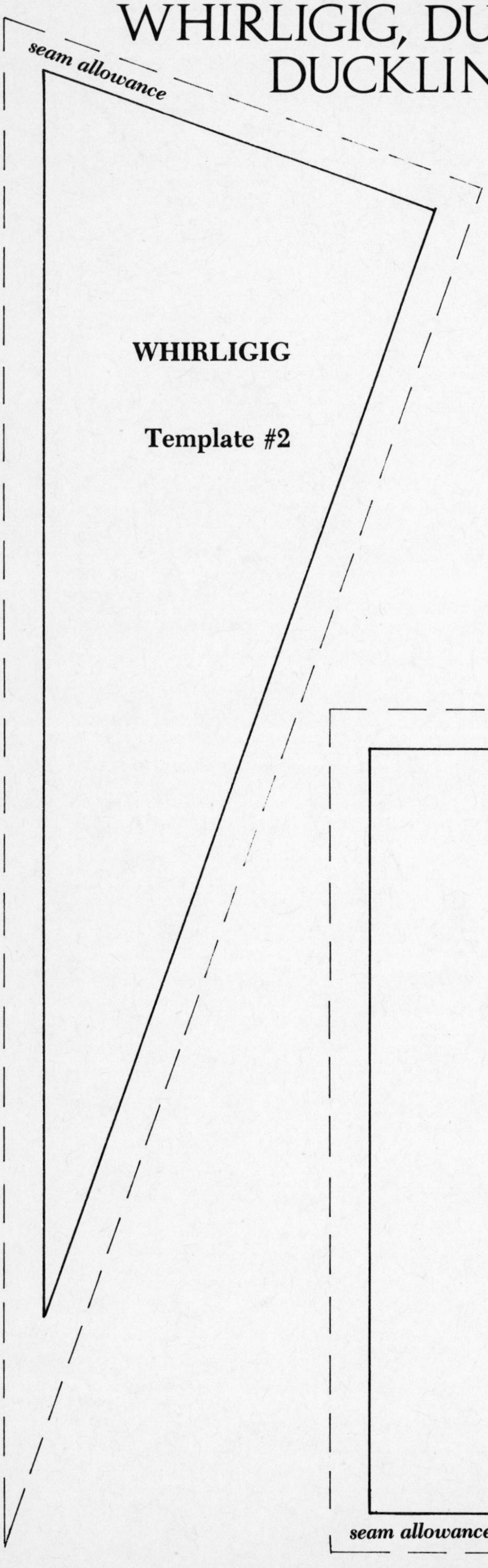

Pattern Pieces For
GIANT TULIP QUILT

PLATE 11

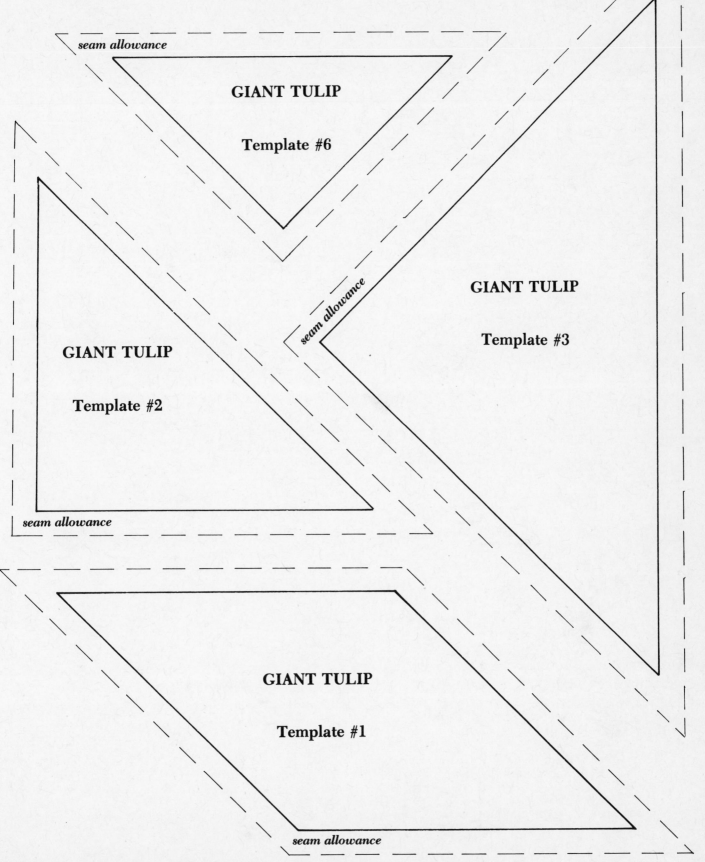

seam allowance

GIANT TULIP

Template #6

seam allowance

GIANT TULIP

Template #3

GIANT TULIP

Template #2

seam allowance

GIANT TULIP

Template #1

seam allowance

PLATE 12

Pattern Pieces For
GIANT TULIP QUILT

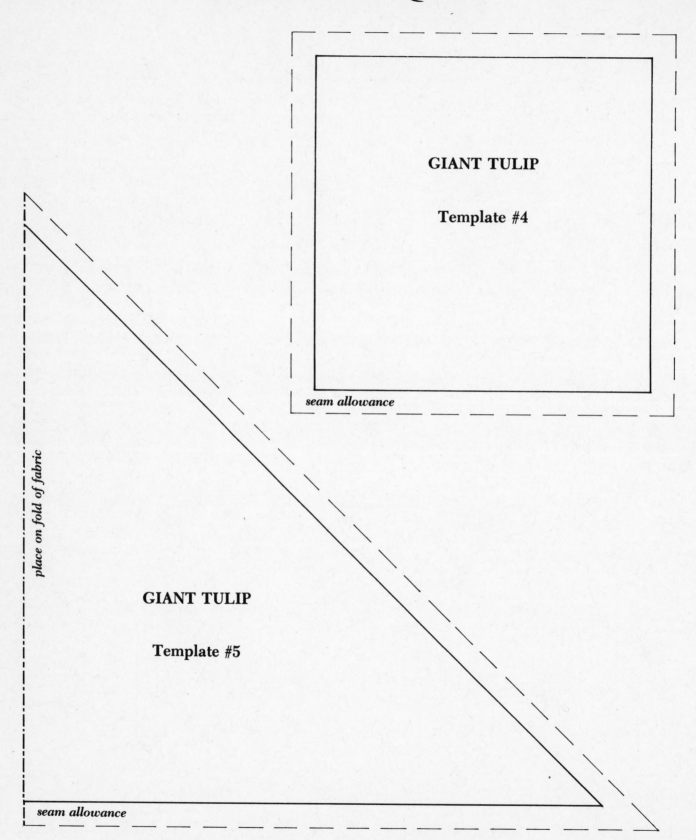

GIANT TULIP

Template #4

seam allowance

place on fold of fabric

GIANT TULIP

Template #5

seam allowance

Pattern Pieces For GIANT TULIP QUILT

PLATE 13

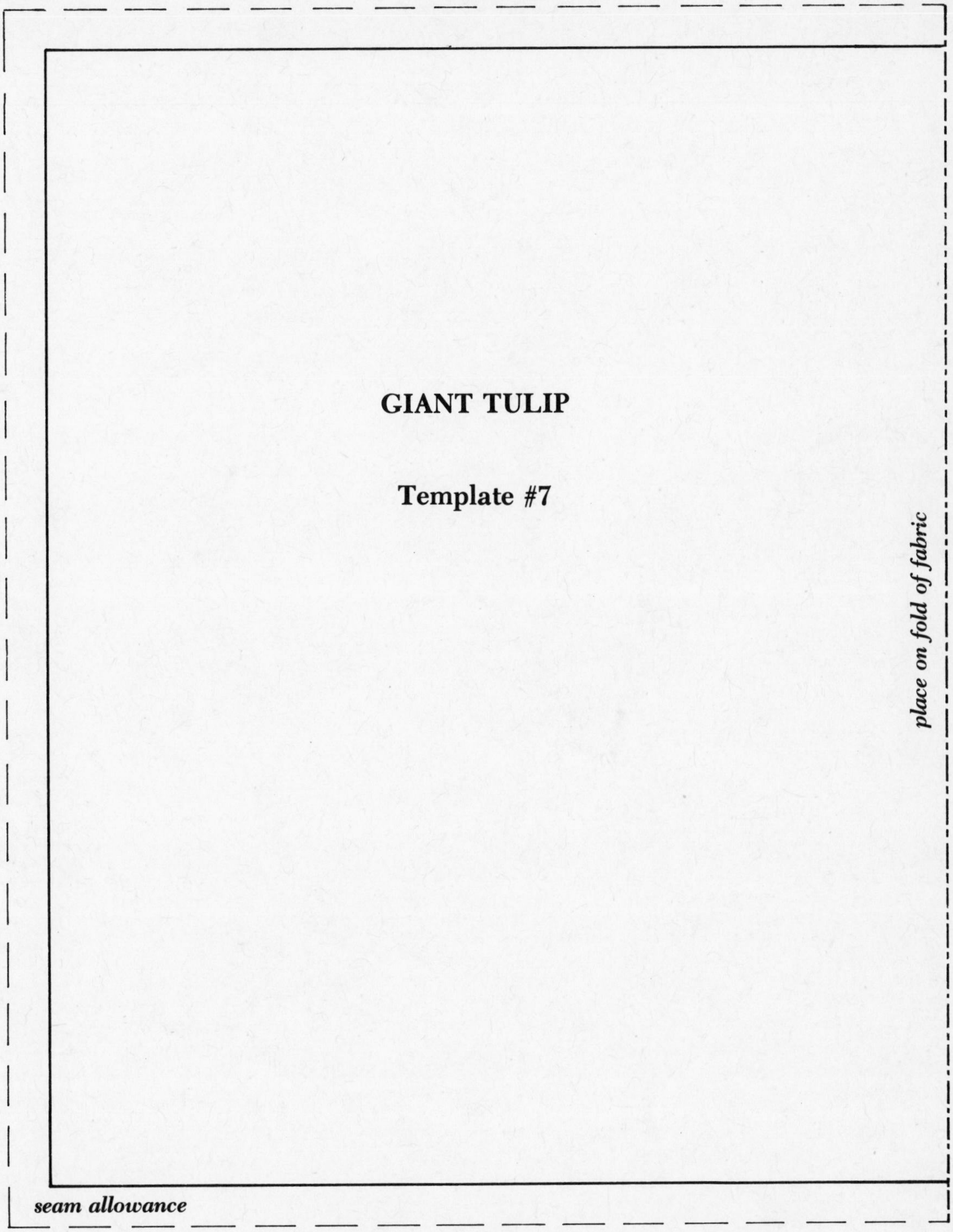
GIANT TULIP
Template #7
place on fold of fabric
seam allowance

PLATE 14

Pattern Pieces For
ROSE OF SHARON WREATH

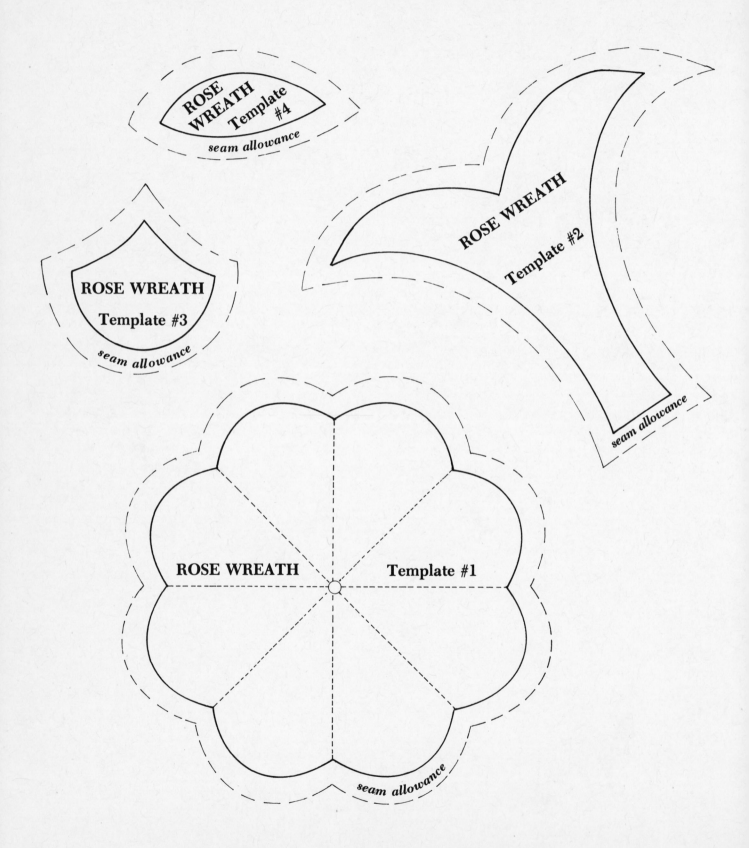

ROSE WREATH
Template #4
seam allowance

ROSE WREATH
Template #2

ROSE WREATH
Template #3
seam allowance

seam allowance

ROSE WREATH   Template #1

seam allowance

Pattern Pieces For
OAK AND ACORN QUILT

PLATE 15

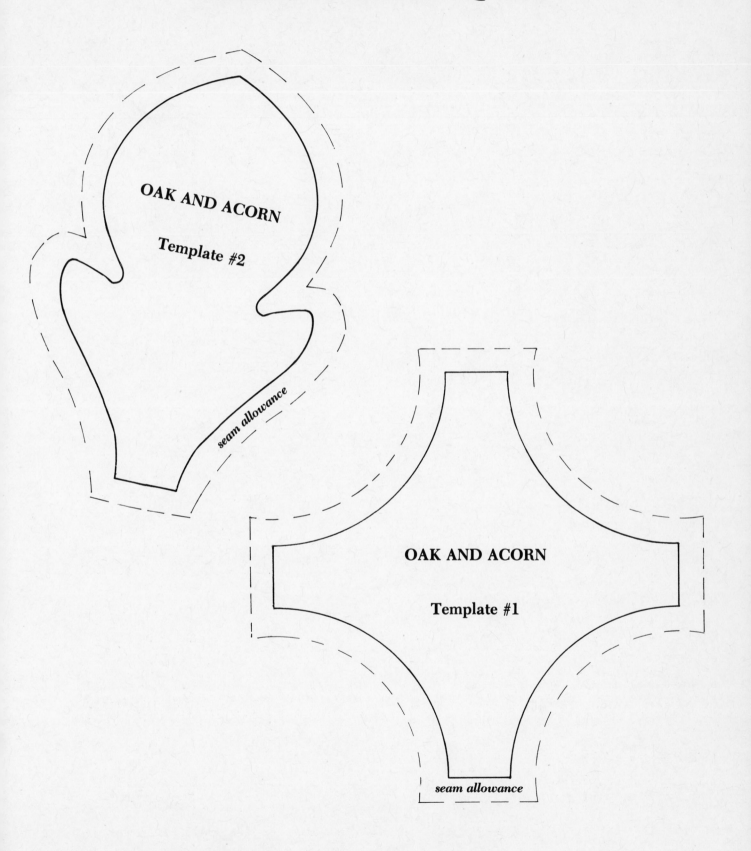

OAK AND ACORN

Template #2

seam allowance

OAK AND ACORN

Template #1

seam allowance

PLATE 16

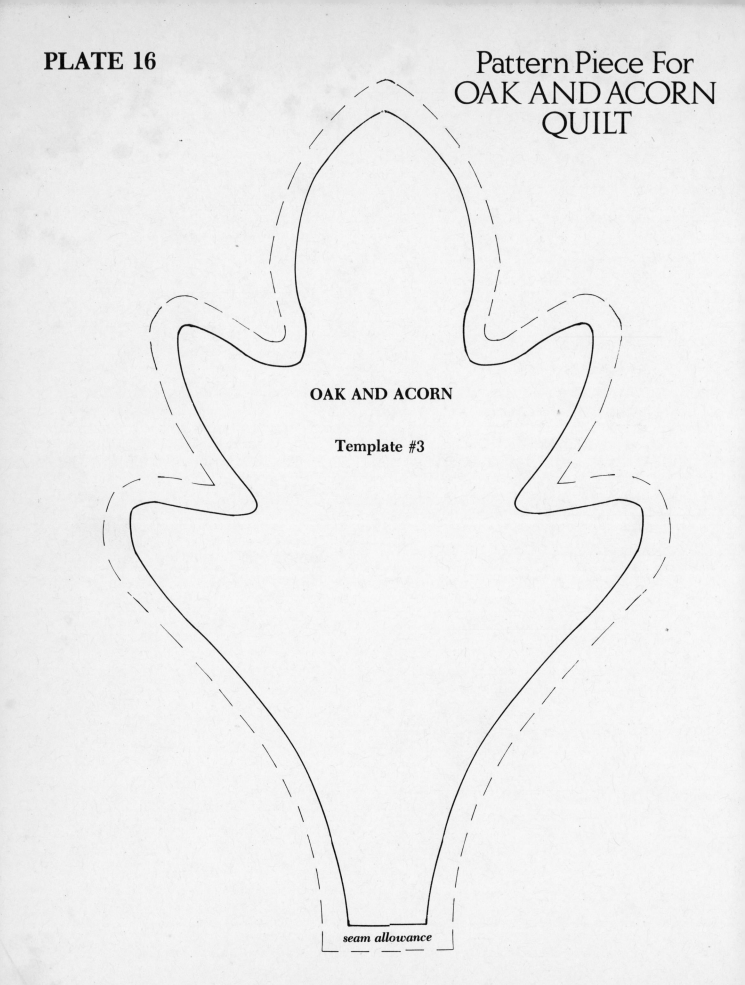

OAK AND ACORN

Template #3

seam allowance